MIRACLE
BREAKTHROUGH
POWER
OF THE FIRST FRUIT

Unleash God's
Astonishing Blessings

DAVE WILLIAMS

MIRACLE
BREAKTHROUGH
POWER
OF THE FIRST FRUIT

MIRACLE BREAKTHROUGH POWER
OF THE FIRST FRUIT

Unless otherwise marked, all Scripture quotations are taken from the King James Version of the Bible.

Scripture quotations marked (NKJV) are from the New King James Version, copyright © 1982 by Thomas Nelson, Inc. Used by permission. All rights reserved.

Scripture quotations marked (NLT) are taken from the Holy Bible, New Living Translation, copyright 1996, 2004. Used by permission of Tyndale House Publishers, Inc., Wheaton, Illinois, 60189. All rights reserved.

Scripture quotations marked (MSG) are taken from The Message, copyright © 1993, 1994, 1995, 1996, 2000, 2001, 2002. Used by permission of NavPress Publishing Group.

Scripture quotations marked (AMP) are taken from the Amplified® Bible, copyright © 1954, 1958, 1962, 1964, 1965, 1987 by The Lockman Foundation. Used by permission. (www.Lockman.org)

Scriptures marked (CEV) are taken from the Contemporary English Version of the Bible, copyright © 1995 by American Bible Society. Used by permission.

Copyright © 2008 by Dr. David R. Williams

ISBN 0-938020-89-7

First Printed 2008

Published by:

DECAPOLIS
PUBLISHING

Printed in the United States of America

OTHER BOOKS BY DAVE WILLIAMS

TABLE OF CONTENTS

"I'm absolutely certain that God would rather see His children be millionaires than the devil's children be millionaires."

1

WHO WANTS TO BE A MILLIONAIRE?

How would you like me to show you a simple way you will be able to . . .

- honor the Lord deeply
- encourage the Lord's servants
- connect to a powerful anointing
- bring God's blessing over your home
- ensure the Lord will be an enemy to your enemies
- bring the destruction of personal adversaries
- release powerful angels on your behalf
- speed up the power of God to heal and give long life

. . . all by one simple act of faith?

WHO WANTS TO BE A MILLIONAIRE?

What is this simple act of faith that can unleash these astonishing blessings?

It's called the *Miracle Breakthrough Power of the First Fruit*. This teaching is for millionaires and future millionaires only. If you are not a millionaire, be one by faith. Call those things that are not as though they are.

> (As it is written, I have made thee a father of many nations,) before him whom he believed, even God, who quickeneth the dead, and calleth those things which be not as though they were.
>
> —Romans 4:17

I'm absolutely certain that God would rather see His children be millionaires than the devil's children be millionaires. Think about it. After all, He's the one who gives us the power to get wealth, even though many either ignore or do not take advantage of that power.

> Remember the LORD your God. He is the one who gives you power to be successful, in order to fulfill the covenant he confirmed to your ancestors with an oath.
>
> —Deuteronomy 8:18 (NLT)

> But thou shalt remember the LORD thy God: for it is he that giveth thee power to get wealth, that he may establish his covenant which He sware unto thy fathers, as it is this day.
>
> —Deuteronomy 8:18

Until recently, I did not understand the practice of the first fruit offering and the overflowing promises of wealth attached to it. I casually equated it with tithing, believing the terms to be synonymous. The teachings I had heard on the first fruit seemed so complicated; I wanted to scream. I just didn't understand it. I even wondered if perhaps this teaching was merely a cleverly designed doctrine created by some greedy preacher. But, I learned something.

TWO THINGS THAT CRIPPLE OUR LEARNING & GROWTH

Over the years, I've learned two things cripple our learning and growth. The first is comfort. When we are comfortable with the familiar, and choose to stay there, we stop growing. The second is arrogance—thinking we already know it. Both situations cripple learning and growth.

I didn't think I was in a comfort zone of some kind because I'm known for stretching the limits. I asked the Lord if maybe I was blinded to some truth. Did I imagine that I already knew it? After all, I had written four books about wealth and abundance after many years of intense research and practice. How could there be something I missed? I wanted to be open hearted to fresh revelation; but, not to some "make the preacher rich" heresy.

I love gospel television, but I've seen some preachers who no longer preach Jesus Christ even though they occasionally allude to Him. I listened as they called their viewers to send in money for a miracle. Each week it's the same old thing: money, money, and more money. They add some isolated Scriptures here and there to lend credibility to their message and convince their viewers that the key to luxury and riches is to send them some money. I can't know their motivation; I do know that my stomach turns when I hear them broadcasting the same old message time and time again.

I don't want to criticize. I don't want a closed heart, but I have a problem with preachers who continually focus on getting money from people.

Thankfully, God looked at my heart's motivation.

Then a miracle of revelation hit me. I was driving to a meeting in Detroit listening to a tape that a friend had given me about the first fruit. I listened to it once, then again, and then a third time. Suddenly, it was as if the light went on. It clicked! At last, I understood. It was like finding the missing link in God's system of wealth.

TYPES OF GIVING

I knew there were four types of giving—seed planting—found in God's Word, each coming with its own set of amazing promises. The four are: the tithe, offerings, alms, and a faith promise. Now I know there is a fifth type of giving: the first fruit.

THE TITHE

The first was the practice of tithing. This is bringing ten percent of your gross income to the Lord's work. It's the foundational principle of God's system for wealth because it breaks financial curses and opens the windows of heaven (Malachi 3:8-13).

Tithing is a principle that extends back before the Law was given (Genesis 14:20; Hebrews 7:6). For many years I had practiced tithing and enjoyed the benefits and promises associated with it.

> **Will a man rob or defraud God? Yet you rob and defraud Me. But you say, In what way do we rob or defraud You? [You have withheld your] tithes and offerings.**
> **You are cursed with the curse, for you are robbing Me, even this whole nation.**
> **Bring all the tithes (the whole tenth of your income) into the storehouse, that there may be food in My house, and prove Me now by it, says the Lord of hosts,**

if I will not open the windows of heaven for you and pour you out a blessing, that there shall not be room enough to receive it.
And I will rebuke the devourer [insects and plagues] for your sakes and he shall not destroy the fruits of your ground, neither shall your vine drop its fruit before the time in the field, says the Lord of hosts.

—Malachi 3:8-11 (AMP)

OFFERINGS

The second principle was the practice of giving offerings. These are gifts we determine to give to God's work beyond the tithe. Like tithing, for many years I gave offerings. This is planting seeds for your future harvest.

My sons, do not neglect your duties any longer! The LORD has chosen you to stand in his presence, to minister to him, and to lead the people in worship and present offerings to Him.

—2 Chronicles 29:11 (NLT)

My scattered people who live beyond the rivers of Ethiopia will come to present their offerings.

—Zephaniah 3:10 (NLT)

Will a man rob God? Yet ye have robbed me. But ye say, Wherein have we robbed thee? In tithes and offerings.

—Malachi 3:8

Now after many years I came to bring alms to my nation, and offerings.

—Acts 24:17

ALMS

The third principle is alms. Alms are "loans" you make to the Lord when you give to the poor, needy, orphans, or widows. It's benevolence and kindness in action. Ever since I can remember in my Christian life, I have given alms to orphanages, the poor, and the needy. When you give to feed a hungry child in a third world country, that's alms. God promises a return on your investment to help others. It's not "seed-planting" for a harvest, but a "loan" to the Lord.

> **If you help the poor, you are lending to the LORD—
> and he will repay you!**
>
> > **—Proverbs 19:17 (NLT)**

> **He who has pity on the poor lends to the LORD,
> And He will pay back what he has given.**
>
> > **—Proverbs 19:17 (NKJV)**

> **And a certain man lame from his mother's womb
> was carried, whom they laid daily at the gate of the
> temple which is called Beautiful, to ask alms of them
> that entered into the temple;
> Who seeing Peter and John about to go into the
> temple asked an alms.**
>
> > **—Acts 3:2-3**

> **There was a certain man in Caesarea called
> Cornelius, a centurion of the band called the Italian
> band,
> A devout man, and one that feared God with all
> his house, which gave much alms to the people, and
> prayed to God alway.**
>
> > **—Acts 10:1-2**

The offering of alms is a benevolent, charitable gift to someone in need. The tithe, however, is the Lord's and goes to the Temple (or church) storehouse. Offerings also go through the temple treasury, as do faith promises for missions. A quick study of each type of giving will show you the clear difference.

THE FAITH PROMISE

The fourth faith-stretching principle is called a "faith promise." In 2 Corinthians 8 and 9 Paul was talking about this principle when he mentioned a group of believers who were giving more than they were able.

> **Now I want you to know, dear brothers and sisters, what God in his kindness has done through the churches in Macedonia.**
> **They are being tested by many troubles, and they are very poor. But they are also filled with abundant joy, which has overflowed in rich generosity.**
> **For I can testify that they gave not only what they could afford, but far more. And they did it of their own free will.**
>
> **—2 Corinthians 8:1-3 (NLT)**

A faith promise is agreeing to allow the Lord to channel money through you to a missionary or missions ministry. You ask God how much he wants you to promise, then, throughout the year, you ask Him to cause it to flow through you until it is paid. This is a real test of whether or not you are ready to handle large amounts of God's wealth. Since 1977, my wife and I have made faith promises for the sake of world missions.

THE FIFTH KEY EMERGES—THE FIRST FRUIT

I had always thought there were were only four kinds of giving: tithes, offerings, alms, and faith promises.

But I was wrong. Now the fresh revelation of a fifth key in God's wealth system was emerging as I drove down the highway toward Detroit. It is called the "first fruit offering," something totally different than tithing, although I had always lumped the two together. Tithing has the power to break financial curses and to open the windows of heaven. The first fruit has the power to break bondages, launch success, destroy enemy assignments against your life, and to bring the blessing over your home.

THE FIRST FRUIT CHANGES EVERYTHING

When I discovered the miracle breakthrough power of the first fruit, everything changed. Oh, I still faced struggles and adversaries, but now I had a fresh miracle breakthrough power to be a "wall-breaker," "city-taker," "earth-shaker," and "legend-maker."

After my first act of faith in exercising the miracle breakthrough power of the first fruit, almost instantly, amazing things began happening to me. I felt that God was pushing me to a higher level of His Spirit and anointing, and shoving me right into the "wealthy place" (Psalm 66:12).

I need to tell you up front, that I don't cherish the idea of sharing this teaching with you. It's not because I don't want you to know about it, but because some will think this teaching is self-serving and will criticize both the teaching and me. It's never a joy when people misunderstand your motivation. But I cannot hold back when God has given me this breakthrough revelation from His Word that has changed the way I do things and brought so many miracle blessings into my home and life.

I'm not trying to get anything from anybody. I have everything I need and more. God has been good to me.

I wish I could express how grateful I am to God for the friend who gave me that tape and for the message on it. I'm thankful that God allowed me to discover another way to honor him with my life and a way to conquer every design of the devil. The miracle breakthrough power of the first fruit is faith in action.

When I returned home, I taught our congregation about the first fruit. The results were miraculous. A fresh wave of faith came over our church and many people testified of new levels of personal prosperity and impressive advancements in their lives. I will tell you more about some of them later in this book.

I want to be clear right from the onset: this teaching is not just about money. It's about obedience. Obedience to God's revealed will and plan is faith in action. And whenever you put action to your faith, you'll soon see miracle results.

Are you ready for a penetrating revelation that could thrust you into the wealthy place? Are you ready for the missing ingredient to real increase? If so, then let's get started.

"If the first is blessed, then all the rest will be blessed."

2

YOUR OVERFLOWING BARNS

I am going to show you something we have misunderstood for years. I am going to offer you something that can bring you breakthrough power, ensure blessings in your home, and link you up with a richer, stronger anointing than you've ever known before.

> **Honour the LORD with thy substance, and with the firstfruits of all thine increase:**
> **So shall thy barns be filled with plenty, and thy presses shall burst out with new wine.**
>
> **—Proverbs 3:9-10**

Let's take a look at these verses and ask some probing questions.

Question 1: What are we to do?

Answer: Honor the Lord. Isn't that the goal of every born again child of God who loves Jesus?

Question 2: How do we honor the Lord?

Answer: We honor the Lord with our substance and with the first fruits of all our increase. Substance is our stuff, our things, our possessions. We understand that. We honor the

Lord with our substance—everything we have. This means we don't have an ownership mentality, but a management mentality. We manage what God has entrusted to us to manage. It's not really ours, although God allows us to manage it. If God says give it, we give it because it is His anyway. In so doing, we honor Him.

We understand what "substance" is, but what about "increase"? What is meant by increase? Even though some translations call it "income," it is NOT income.

We've often used this as a tithing verse, saying we must bring the first fruit of all our income to the Lord. But this is not a verse about tithing. It's about something different—something with amazing promises attached to it.

THE AMAZING PROMISES

Question 3: What is the promise to us if we honor the Lord this way?

Answer: "So shall thy barns be filled with plenty and thy presses shall burst with new wine." Read it from the Amplified Bible, "Honor the Lord with your capital and sufficiency from righteous labors and with the first fruits of all your income." Here it does say, income, but in the Hebrew language it is increase. Now I understand, as you do, that some people's income is their increase. For example, when you're living on a fixed income from investments, or when you're living solely on the interest or gain of investments, your increase and income are the same things.

So shall your storage places be filled with plenty. . . .
—Proverbs 3:10a

22

Question 4: *Where do you store your money?*

Answer: You store money in storage places for money. We call them banks or investment vehicles such as stocks, bonds, mutual funds, or real estate. When we honor the Lord with the first fruit, He promises that our storage places will be filled with plenty.

FIRST FRUIT—A PROMISE TO COME

After I listened to the teaching on the first fruit, I wanted to study the concept—not just biblically—but historically as well. I always want to research new revelation both biblically and historically. I discovered that to the Hebrew people, the word "first fruit" (it was one word—firstfruit—in the Hebrew language) meant a promise to come. The practice of giving a first fruit offering was something they did, related to a promise that was going to come. In fact, none of the harvest could be enjoyed until the first fruit was offered.

Did you know that Jesus Christ rose from the dead on the Feast of the First Fruits? It was not called Easter, it was called the day of the Feast of the First Fruits. In fact, when Jesus died on the cross, the tombs of some of the dead saints opened up and they began to walk around. It was the first fruit resurrection (Matthew 27:52, 53; 1 Corinthians 15:20-23).

> **And the graves were opened; and many bodies of the saints which slept arose,**
> **And came out of the graves after his resurrection, and went into the holy city, and appeared unto many.**
> **—Matthew 27:52-53**

23

> But now is Christ risen from the dead, and become
> the firstfruits of them that slept.
> For since by man came death, by man came also the
> resurrection of the dead.
> For as in Adam all die, even so in Christ shall all be
> made alive.
> But every man in his own order: Christ the first-
> fruits; afterward they that are Christ's at his coming.
>
> —1 Corinthians 15:20-23

IF THE FIRST IS HOLY, THE REST WILL BE HOLY TOO

Now, this is an incredibly important principle to understand. Let's look at Romans 11:16 from two translations, the King James Version and the Contemporary English Version.

> For if the firstfruit be holy, the lump is also holy:
> and if the root be holy, so are the branches.
>
> —Romans 11:16

> If part of a batch of dough is made holy by being
> offered to God, then all of the dough is holy. If the
> roots of a tree are holy, the rest of the tree is holy too.
>
> —Romans 11:16 (CEV)

In other words, whatever happens to the first is going to happen to the rest. If you receive an increase of some sort and that first increase is blessed, then all the rest of your increase is going to be blessed.

If the first is holy, the whole lump is holy. If the first is blessed, the rest will be blessed. This is a spiritual principle.

EXAMPLE OF THE FIRST FRUIT

If you are a car manufacturer, the first car that comes off the line should go to an anointed person of God as a first fruit offering. The first car is the first fruit, and you should get it to a man or woman of God so all the rest of your cars will be blessed. You want the first to be a blessing, so the rest can be blessed.

If I owned a car dealership, and I wanted my dealership blessed, I would give the first new car that rolled onto my lot to a man or woman of God so that the rest of my sales all year long would be blessed. If the first is blessed, then all the rest will be blessed.

Bob Harrison leads an international ministry that motivates thousands to reach their greatest potential. He conducts "increase events" in Florida, California, and Hawaii with top-notch speakers and master motivators—like Bob himself. Check out his website at www.increase.org.

Back in the 1970s, Bob took over a dying Chrysler dealership in southern California. It was during the height of the recession when gas was being rationed. Knowing the first thing he had to do, he got on the phone with his pastor and asked him if he would like a new car now and every six months thereafter. Why did he do this?

Bob knew the secret of the first fruit offering. Within months, the dealership's business skyrocketed into the top ten in sales. With God's help, through the miracle breakthrough power of the first fruit and some good business savvy, Bob turned that nearly bankrupt dealership into a winning business despite the odds against him.

IF THE FIRST IS BLESSED, THE REST WILL BE BLESSED

The first fruit needs to be offered because if the first is blessed the rest will be blessed. It's a spiritual principle. And, as we shall see, the first fruit is not the same as the tithe. The tithe went to the temple (or church) treasury. The first fruit was an offering that always went to the priest or Levite personally. It was given to ensure the first of the increase would be holy so the rest would be holy and blessed.

Over the past several years, I've planted first fruit offerings in a number of ministries to make a connection with leaders who had gifts or an anointing that I wanted. When I was given a check for attending a meeting in Detroit, it was the first time I had ever been paid for that. It was the first of a new income. So I sent the entire amount to the teacher whom God anointed and used to impart the revelation of the first fruit offering to me. It was his message I listened to on the way to that meeting.

I have given first fruit offerings to seven ministries, each with a different anointing. The results have been dramatic. I've had greater opportunities than ever before to present the Gospel and speak God's Word in large settings; my honorariums have increased, empty rental investment properties have filled up, and I've broken through a serious financial barrier.

Mary Jo, my precious wife, received an inheritance check for $1,800.00. It was the first portion of an inheritance from her mother's estate. I wondered what we would do with it (and I had some wonderful ideas).

Then she asked, "Isn't this the first time we ever got an inheritance check?"

"Yes," I responded.

"Then, shouldn't I give it as a first fruit?"

"Yes, honey, you're right. You want to keep the blessing over our home, and you want the rest of our things to be blessed."

She sent the money to an anointed woman's ministry for her personal use. She did not expect a tax deduction. She gave it simply to bless a woman of God and get a connection with her anointing. Mary Jo is a sweet woman with a tender heart, and she wants to have the anointing of speaking boldly. So, she sent the first fruit—all $1,800.00—to a boldly speaking woman minister.

When you want the miracle breakthrough power of the first fruit activated in your life, find a servant of God you respect, someone who has an anointing you want in your life, and give the first to him or her. I'll explain more as we continue in the next chapter.

"When you plant seeds of any kind, you must have both good seed and good soil to get a good harvest."

3

PATTERN AND PROMISES OF THE FIRST FRUIT

Let me briefly explain the pattern for the miracle break-through power of the first fruit. This will be a brief overview which I will explain in greater detail later. The following highlights are taken from Exodus 13, Exodus 23, Leviticus 23, Numbers 18, Deuteronomy 26:10, 2 Kings 4, 2 Chronicles 31, Nehemiah 10 and 12, Ezekiel 20, 44, and 48, Proverbs 3:9-10, and Romans 11:16.

1. *The first fruit is the first and the best; it's a portion.*

And the feast of harvest, the firstfruits of thy labours, which thou hast sown in the field: and the feast of ingathering, which is in the end of the year, when thou hast gathered in thy labours out of the field.

—Exodus 23:16

The first of the firstfruits of thy land thou shalt bring into the house of the LORD thy God.

—Exodus 23:19a

Speak unto the children of Israel, and say unto them, When ye be come into the land which I give unto you, and shall reap the harvest thereof, then ye

> shall bring a sheaf of the firstfruits of your harvest
> unto the priest.
>
> —Leviticus 23:10

> All the best of the oil, and all the best of the wine,
> and of the wheat, the firstfruits of them which they
> shall offer unto the LORD, them have I given thee.
>
> —Numbers 18:12

2.   *The first fruit is not the tithe. The tithe is ten percent; the first fruit is the first.*

> And as soon as the commandment came abroad, the
> children of Israel brought in abundance the first-
> fruits of corn, wine, and oil, and honey, and of all the
> increase of the field; and the tithe of all things brought
> they in abundantly.
>
> —2 Chronicles 31:5

[Note: The tithe and the first fruit were clearly two different offerings.]

3.   *The first fruit is a gift to a man or woman of God, or someone who is serving the Lord in some kind of ministry.*

> All the first crops of their land that the people pres-
> ent to the LORD belong to you [speaking of the priests].
> Any member of your family who is ceremonially clean
> may eat this food
>
> —Numbers 18:13 (NLT)

[Note: The tithe belongs to the Lord. The first fruit offering belongs to the priest or man of God. The priests and Levites had a salary of about one third of whatever the tithe was. The first fruit was an additional "appreciation" gift to honor and worship the Lord by encouraging the man of God.]

> **The firstfruits of your grain, of your new wine, and of your oil, and the first or best of the fleece of your sheep you shall give the priest.**
>
> **—Deuteronomy 18:4 (AMP)**

[Note: The first fruit was given to the priest, the man of God].

> **And now, behold, I have brought the firstfruits of the land, which thou, O LORD, hast given me. And thou shalt set it before the LORD thy God, and worship before the LORD thy God:**
>
> **—Deuteronomy 26:10**

[Note: Giving a first fruit offering to a man or woman of God is an act of worshiping and honoring the Lord.]

4. The first fruit is not given because the priest or Levite (minister) needs it. It is given out of obedience and to get a connection with the recipient's anointing.

> **The people of Israel responded immediately and generously by bringing the first of their crops and grain, new wine, olive oil, honey, and all the produce of their fields. They brought a large quantity—a tithe of all they produced.**
>
> **—2 Chronicles 31:5 (NLT)**

[Note once again: The tithe and the first fruit were clearly two different offerings.]

> **On the day they were anointed, the LORD commanded the Israelites to give these portions to the priests as their permanent share from generation to generation.**
>
> **—Leviticus 7:36 (NLT)**

> **And the LORD spake unto Aaron, Behold, I also have given thee the charge of mine heave offerings of all the hallowed things of the children of Israel; unto**

> thee have I given them by reason of the anointing, and
> to thy sons, by an ordinance for ever.
>
> —Numbers 18:8

> [I thank my God] for your fellowship (your sympa-
> thetic cooperation and contributions and partnership)
> in advancing the good news (the Gospel) from the first
> day [you heard it] until now.
>
> —Philippians 1:5 (AMP)

I need to comment here. Even though some teachers use Leviticus 7 and Numbers 18 as "proof texts" for the connection with a man of God's anointing, I honestly believe it is a stretch to squeeze that meaning out of these verses. To me, these verses seem to be talking about the priest's anointing, not referring to a "connection" or "impartation" to one who brings a gift. However, the "connection with the anointing" principle is true.

For example, Paul told the Philippians they became partners with him (connected to him) when they gave to bless him in his ministry. Also, when you plant seeds of any kind, you must have both good seed and good soil to get a good harvest. Thus, when you plant a seed in the life of an anointed man or woman of God, you get the same kind of harvest. In a spiritual sense, you get a connection with their anointing. I'll expand on this principle in chapter seven.

5. *The first fruit (sometimes called "the heave offering") is given, and the recipient waves it before the Lord to make it acceptable and to bring the blessing over the giver's home.*

> And ye shall count unto you from the morrow after
> the sabbath, from the day that ye brought the sheaf of
> the wave offering;
>
> —Leviticus 23:15a

> And the priest shall wave them with the bread of the
> firstfruits for a wave offering before the LORD, with
> the two lambs: they shall be holy to the LORD for the
> priest.
>
> —Leviticus 23:20

> And the first of all the firstfruits of all things, and
> every oblation of all, of every sort of your oblations,
> shall be the priest's: ye shall also give unto the priest
> the first of your dough, that he may cause the blessing
> to rest in thine house.
>
> —Ezekiel 44:30

Look at this amazing promise for giving a first fruit offering unto the priest (a man or woman of God, or someone
whose anointing you'd like a connection with): "he shall cause
THE blessing to rest in your house." How many homes today
really have THE blessing resting in them?

*6. When the first fruit is given, the rest of your in-
crease is blessed. Remember, what happens to the first, happens to the rest.*

> For if the firstfruit be holy, the lump is also holy:
> and if the root be holy, so are the branches.
>
> —Romans 11:16

*7. The first fruit is offered to encourage a man or
woman of God and to help free them financially so they can
focus on the Word and work of God.*

> Moreover he commanded the people that dwelt in
> Jerusalem to give the portion of the priests and the
> Levites, that they might be encouraged in the law of
> the LORD.
> And as soon as the commandment came abroad, the
> children of Israel brought in abundance the first-
> fruits of corn, wine, and oil, and honey, and of all the

increase of the field; and the tithe of all things brought
they in abundantly.

—2 Chronicles 31:4-5

8. *The first fruit, when it is offered in faith, (1) sends
the Angel of the Lord ahead of you; (2) makes God an enemy to your enemies; (3) overthrows your adversaries, and
(4) brings the power of healing and health.*

The first of the firstfruits of thy land thou shalt
bring into the house of the LORD thy God. Thou
shalt not seethe a kid in his mother's milk.

Behold, I send an Angel before thee, to keep thee in
the way, and to bring thee into the place which I have
prepared.

Beware of him, and obey his voice, provoke him
not; for he will not pardon your transgressions: for
my name is in him.

But if thou shalt indeed obey his voice, and do
all that I speak; then I will be an enemy unto thine
enemies, and an adversary unto thine adversaries.

For mine Angel shall go before thee, and bring
thee in unto the Amorites, and the Hittites, and the
Perizzites, and the Canaanites, the Hivites, and the
Jebusites: and I will cut them off.

Thou shalt not bow down to their gods, nor serve
them, nor do after their works: but thou shalt utterly
overthrow them, and quite break down their images.

And ye shall serve the LORD your God, and he shall
bless thy bread, and thy water; and I will take sickness
away from the midst of thee.

There shall nothing cast their young, nor be barren,
in thy land: the number of thy days I will fulfill.

I will send my fear before thee, and will destroy all
the people to whom thou shalt come, and I will make
all thine enemies turn their backs unto thee.

—Exodus 23:19-27

[Note: In other words, your enemies will run from you!]

And I will send hornets before thee, which shall
drive out the Hivite, the Canaanite, and the Hittite,
from before thee.

—Exodus 23:28

[Note: The word "hornets" was used to signify "terror."
God will terrorize your enemies.]

**9. *The first fruit offering brings the promise of over-
flowing storehouses and fresh revelation (new wine).***

Honour the LORD with thy substance, and with
the firstfruits of all thine increase:
So shall thy barns be filled with plenty, and thy
presses shall burst out with new wine.

—Proverbs 3:9-10

**10. *The first fruit brings the blessing over your home
and ensures the promise you are looking for will come.***

The first of the ripe fruits and all the gifts brought
to the LORD will go to the priests. The first samples
of each grain harvest and the first of your flour must
also be given to the priests so the LORD will bless your
homes.

—Ezekiel 44:30 (NLT)

11. *The first fruit honors the Lord.*

Honour the LORD with thy substance, and with
the firstfruits of all thine increase:

—Proverbs 3:9

And now, behold, I have brought the firstfruits of
the land, which thou, O LORD, hast given me. And
thou shalt set it before the LORD thy God, and worship before the LORD thy God:

—Deuteronomy 26:10

[Note: Once again, we see that giving a first fruit offering to a man or woman of God is an act of worshiping and honoring the Lord.]

Now that we've laid a good foundation, I'm going to take you through many Scriptures because I want to show you that the first fruit offering is a pattern in God's Word. We're going to see how much of our success is tied to the first fruit and how it relates to our receiving breakthrough miracles.

"When the children of Israel were in bondage and then offered the first fruit, that's when their bondage was broken."

4

RELEASE FROM BONDAGE

The Bible mentions the word "tithe" 32 times, and it also mentions the word "firstfruit" 32 times. Let's start a shtudy of these words in Exodus.

> And the LORD spake unto Moses, saying,
> Sanctify unto me all the firstborn, whatsoever openeth the womb among the children of Israel, both of man and of beast: it is mine.
> And Moses said unto the people, Remember this day, in which ye came out from Egypt, out of the house of bondage; for by strength of hand the LORD brought you out from this place: there shall no leavened bread be eaten.
> This day came ye out in the month Abib.
> And it shall be when the LORD shall bring thee into the land of the Canaanites, and the Hittites, and the Amorites, and the Hivites, and the Jebusites, which he sware unto thy fathers to give thee, a land flowing with milk and honey, that thou shalt keep this service in this month.
> Seven days thou shalt eat unleavened bread, and in the seventh day shall be a feast to the LORD.
> Unleavened bread shall be eaten seven days; and there shall no leavened bread be seen with thee, neither shall there be leaven seen with thee in all thy quarters.

And thou shalt shew thy son in that day, saying,
This is done because of that which the LORD did unto
me when I came forth out of Egypt.

And it shall be for a sign unto thee upon thine
hand, and for a memorial between thine eyes, that the
LORD's law may be in thy mouth: for with a strong
hand hath the LORD brought thee out of Egypt.

Thou shalt therefore keep this ordinance in his
season from year to year.

And it shall be when the LORD shall bring thee
into the land of the Canaanites, as he sware unto thee
and to thy fathers, and shall give it thee,

That thou shalt set apart unto the LORD all that
openeth the matrix, and every firstling that cometh
of a beast which thou hast; the males shall be the
LORD's.

And every firstling of an ass thou shalt redeem with
a lamb; and if thou wilt not redeem it, then thou shalt
break his neck: and all the firstborn of man among
thy children shalt thou redeem.

—Exodus 13:1-13

RELEASE THE FIRST FRUIT FOR RELEASE FROM BONDAGE

God was beginning to teach His children about the miracle breakthrough power of the first fruit. "Redeem" simply means that you bring a valuable offering to the Lord instead of sacrificing your firstborn son. God wanted the first, but didn't want the children sacrificed like animals.

So the people of God provided a first fruit of sorts. But the people of Egypt did not. This meant deliverance to God's people and judgment on their captors.

When you read "the hand of the Lord" as you do in verse three, it means the same thing as "the anointing of the Lord."

Often in Scriptures, when you read "the hand of the Lord" was on someone, it is speaking of the anointing.

> **And it shall be when thy son asketh thee in time to come, saying, What is this? that thou shalt say unto him, By strength of hand the LORD brought us out from Egypt, from the house of bondage:**
>
> **—Exodus 13:14**

THE FIRST FRUIT BREAKS BONDAGES

The Bible says the whole concept of the first fruit is involved in bringing us out of bondage. God said when your children start asking you why you give the first of every-thing—like the first pay raise on your paycheck—as a first fruit offering, your answer is, "Well, I do it because *when* I do, God will break bondages in my life."

When the children of Israel were in bondage and then offered their first fruit, that's when the bondage was broken. Those who did not offer a first fruit suffered a terrible season of shocking and painful loss.

WHAT "PHARAOH" ARE YOU FACING?

> **And it came to pass, when Pharaoh would hardly let us go . . . .**
>
> **—Exodus 13:15a**

"Pharaoh" could be anything according to your situation. Your "Pharaoh" could be a lack, a shortage, a debt, a sickness, a bondage, or some other adversity. You could say, "When debt would hardly let us go," or "when shortage would hardly let us go," or "when poverty and lack would hardly let us go."

> **. . . that the LORD slew all the firstborn in the land of Egypt, both the firstborn of man, and the firstborn**

> **of beast: therefore I sacrifice to the LORD all that
> openeth the matrix, being males; but all the firstborn
> of my children I redeem.**
>
> **—Exodus 13:15b**

The Lord, through the breakthrough power of the first fruit, brought His people out of bondage healthy and wealthy.

I'm going to show you in Scripture how the first fruit offering actually initiates the blessing over your home, the anointing on your life, and how it even relates to introducing the healing power of God to your personal situation.

You'll see how the first fruit can break bondages, entrapments, and enslavements.

The Psalmist recalls this event and tells us that there was no feeble person among them and that they were wealthy. Imagine that. They were enslaved, bound by Pharaoh, and on the very day of their deliverance they came out wealthy and healthy. Not one pair of shoes wore out in 40 years. Everything they had lasted, and the Psalmist says there was not one feeble person among them—not one!

> **The LORD brought his people out of Egypt, loaded
> with silver and gold; and not one among the tribes of
> Israel even stumbled.**
> **Egypt was glad when they were gone, for they feared
> them greatly.**
>
> **—Psalm 105:37-38 (NLT)**

All the wealth of Egypt was given to them, the silver and the gold. Finally the Egyptians screamed, "Get out of here!" Their enemy and tormentor actually commanded them to "Get out of here. Go!"

The miracle breakthrough power of the first fruit is exciting! Are you ready for more?

"A poverty spirit will hold people back from success."

5

GOD WILL BE AN ENEMY TO YOUR ENEMIES

Now it gets really exciting.

God will actually be an enemy to your enemies and an adversary to your adversaries when you launch into the miracle breakthrough power of the first fruit.

We're going to see how the first fruit sets the stage for increase and even real estate. Let's look at Exodus:

> **And the feast of harvest, the firstfruits of thy labours, which thou hast sown in the field: and the feast of ingathering, which is in the end of the year, when thou hast gathered in thy labours out of the field.**
> **Three times in the year all thy males shall appear before the LORD God.**
> **Thou shalt not offer the blood of my sacrifice with leavened bread; neither shall the fat of my sacrifice remain until the morning.**
> **The first of the firstfruits of thy land thou shalt bring into the house of the LORD thy God.**
> **—Exodus 23:16-19a**

Notice they brought the first fruits to the house of the Lord. As we progress in our study, you'll see the first fruits were brought to those who served in the house of the Lord.

> Behold, I send an Angel before thee, to keep thee in
> the way, and to bring thee into the place which I have
> prepared.
>
> —Exodus 23:20

It starts with the first fruit; then, it's like a chain reaction. After bringing the first fruits, God sends an Angel ahead of you to (1) protect you from going the wrong way, and (2) to bring you to the place he has prepared for you.

THE WEALTHY PLACE IS PREPARED FOR YOU!

Now in speaking of these people, Psalm 66:12 tells us about the place God had prepared for them, and for us! Look at it in three different translations:

> . . . we went through fire and through water: but
> thou broughtest us out into a wealthy place.
>
> —Psalm 66:12b

> We went through fire and flood, but you brought us
> to a place of great abundance.
>
> —Psalm 66:12b (NLT)

> We traveled through fire and through floods, but
> you brought us to a land of plenty.
>
> —Psalm 66:12b (CEV)

They cried, "We went through the fire, we went through the flood, and thou (the Lord) brought us into the wealthy place." There's a place God has prepared for you called "the wealthy place." Essentially, He promised, "When you offer this first fruit, I'm going to send an angel ahead of you to make sure you get to the place I've prepared for you. What is that place? It's the "wealthy place."

Beware of him, and obey his voice, provoke him not; for he will not pardon your transgressions: for my name is in him.

But if thou shalt indeed obey his voice, and do all that I speak; then I will be an enemy unto thine enemies, and an adversary unto thine adversaries.

For mine Angel shall go before thee, and bring thee in unto the Amorites, and the Hittites, and the Perizzites, and the Canaanites, the Hivites, and the Jebusites: and I will cut them off.

Thou shalt not bow down to their gods, nor serve them, nor do after their works: but thou shalt utterly overthrow them, and quite break down their images.

And ye shall serve the LORD your God, and he shall bless thy bread, and thy water; and I will take sickness away from the midst of thee.

There shall nothing cast their young, nor be barren, in thy land: the number of thy days I will fulfill.

I will send my fear before thee, and will destroy all the people to whom thou shalt come, and I will make all thine enemies turn their backs unto thee.

And I will send hornets before thee, which shall drive out the Hivite, the Canaanite, and the Hittite, from before thee.

I will not drive them out from before thee in one year; lest the land become desolate, and the beast of the field multiply against thee.

By little and little I will drive them out from before thee, until thou be increased, and inherit the land.

And I will set thy bounds from the Red sea even unto the sea of the Philistines, and from the desert unto the river: for I will deliver the inhabitants of the land into your hand; and thou shalt drive them out before thee.

—**Exodus 23:21-31**

The Word continues in Exodus 23 and God adds these promises:

1. Verse 25—Sickness will be taken from the midst of you.

2. Verse 26—Long life is guaranteed.

3. Verse 27—God will send fear on your enemies and their backs will turn to you. Why? Because they'll be running from you.

4. Verse 28—God will send the "hornet" on your adversaries (referring to the terror of the Lord).

5. Verse 30—You are going to enjoy increase and inherit some land.

The first fruit offering initiates the promise of both increase and land. What is land? Land is real estate. Could you use some real estate? Or, could you use some *more* real estate?

Do you realize that it's the meek that shall inherit the real estate (Matthew 5:5)?

BREAKING THE SPIRIT OF POVERTY

> And the Lord said to Moses,
> Tell the Israelites, When you have come into the land I give you and reap its harvest, you shall bring the sheaf of the firstfruits of your harvest to the priest.
> And he shall wave the sheaf before the Lord,
> that you may be accepted; on the next day after the Sabbath the priest shall wave it [before the Lord].
> —Leviticus 23:9-11 (AMP)

One thing that hinders people from receiving this teaching about the first fruit is a poverty spirit. If the Church ever needed to break any spirit in this day and age, it's the poverty spirit.

God is teaching us how to get into the wealthy place, not just so we can drive a Cadillac or a Mercedes, but so we have money to use with a mission (Deuteronomy 8:18).

Let's look at these same verses from Leviticus in the King James Version:

> And the LORD spake unto Moses, saying,
> Speak unto the children of Israel, and say unto them, When ye be come into the land which I give unto you, and shall reap the harvest thereof, then ye shall bring a sheaf of the firstfruits of your harvest unto the priest:
> And he shall wave the sheaf [portion] before the LORD, to be accepted for you; [to make sure it is accepted with God's blessing] on the morrow after the sabbath the priest shall wave it [brackets mine].
> —Leviticus 23:9-11

These verses instruct how a first fruit offering is to be treated. When a person brings a first fruit offering, the recipient (whoever receives it) should wave it before the Lord and pray something like this, "Lord accept this offering, and may my anointing be on the person who gave this first fruit. May their home be blessed, may their enemies turn their backs and run from them. May sickness be taken away from the midst of them and, Lord, may they have a connection with my life and Yours as well."

Do you know what keeps preachers from preaching like this? The spirit of fear. The preacher is afraid of what people will think.

I read a great book by an African-American youth, Farrah Gray, who was a millionaire by the time he was fourteen years old. He was raised on public assistance. He said that in the projects where he lived there was no lack of creativity, there was no lack of brains, there was no lack of intelligence, there was only a lack of hope. However, his grandmother gave him hope that he could achieve something great. So he started by mixing lotions together and going door-to-door to sell them. He sold them for $1.50 a jar. One woman gave him $5.00 for a jar of lotion. He said, "I don't have any change." She smiled and said, "I didn't ask for any change. I think you're going places, so just consider it an investment in your life."

Next, he invented a new kind of syrup for pancakes and waffles. It was strawberry and vanilla flavored. At the age of thirteen he started the "Way-Out Foods Company." And by the time he was 14 he had sold so much pancake syrup that a major company bought him out to get the rights to use the recipe for his strawberry-vanilla syrup for pancakes.

Fourteen years old and he had become a millionaire!

Now he's written a book. I saw it in the store and bought two copies, one for me and one for my daughter. The name of his book is *Reallionaire.*

A poverty spirit will hold people back from success. A person with a poverty spirit will talk like this: "I get just a little bit as it is, and I'm going to keep it all. And I'm not letting any of my money go to any man of God. I'm not going to make any preacher rich. I don't think a man of God should have more than me." That's an example of a poverty spirit and a spirit of fear.

But, you are different. You are going to get on the leading edge of life through the miracle breakthrough power of the first fruit. Yes, you'll be persecuted when God blesses and prospers you. Jesus promised that in Mark 10:30. But as nationally known teacher of God's prosperity principles, Dr. Leroy Thompson says, "It's not hard to be persecuted as long as you get the deposit to the bank."

THE FIRST ONE IS A FIRST FRUIT

The first one of everything belongs to the Lord. Now what does that mean? Let's say you get a pay raise of $5,200.00 and you're paid every week. Your first paycheck you say, "Oh boy! I've got a hundred dollars extra." No, that $100 is the first fruit. It is the first of your increase. It is the first increase you receive that year. It is the first, not the tithe.

The first fruit is the first of something; the first product you manufacture, the first deal you make, the first commission you earn on a sale, the first harvest from your garden.

It is not the tithe, it is the first fruit. Someone may say, "Dr. Williams, I don't know if I want to do that." Well, it's your choice. I'm not telling you that you have to do anything. I'm just laying a biblical truth out for you. It's up to you to decide how to use this information.

MY PREDICTION

My prediction is that some of you reading this book are going to grab hold of this concept. As a result, God is going to bring you to a place He's been trying to take you to for years. It's called the "wealthy place." There will be some people living on public assistance, living in the housing developments or on a fixed income, and God's going to make you a millionaire or multi-millionaire. God is going to give you a new anointing for breakthrough miracles through the miracle breakthrough power of the first fruit.

"If you cannot be trusted with earthly wealth, how can you be trusted with true spiritual wealth?"

6

IS THE FIRST FRUIT
THE SAME AS THE
TITHE?

Biblically speaking, there is a clear distinction between the first fruit and the tithe.

The tithe is a tenth. The first fruit is the first portion.

The tithe goes to the storehouse. The first fruit goes to a servant of God.

The tithe is a tenth, whether from good money or bad (Leviticus 27:32). The first fruit is the first portion of the best.

The first fruit is the first of whatever increases you get in life. It's the first thing you make to sell, the first commission on a sale, or the first pay raise of the year on your weekly or bi-weekly check.

What if you get a $4000 bonus? I asked the Lord about this, and believe this is appropriate: If you get a $4000 bonus, and you are paid every two weeks, you take that $4000 bonus and divide it by 26 pay periods; that's your first fruit offering. It's the first of your first pay period, whatever that bonus would amount to in your first pay period, that's the first fruit.

That's not the tithe, that's the first fruit offering and the first fruit offering is the offering that breaks the bondage. It's the offering that gets you through to the deliverance you need. Leviticus 27 talks about the tithe.

> **And all the tithe of the land, whether of the seed of the land, or of the fruit of the tree, is the LORD's: it is holy unto the LORD.**
> **And if a man will at all redeem ought of his tithes, he shall add thereto the fifth part thereof.**
> **And concerning the tithe of the herd, or of the flock, even of whatsoever passeth under the rod, the tenth shall be holy unto the LORD.**
> **He shall not search whether it be good or bad, neither shall he change it: and if he change it at all, then both it and the change thereof shall be holy; it shall not be redeemed.**
> **—Leviticus 27: 30-33**

We have no option about the ten percent. It belongs to the Lord. Period. Everyone is given ten percent more than we deserve. And ten percent of all of our income, everything that comes to us, belongs to the Lord. It's not ours.

Driving a Cursed Car?

There are some people who drive cars that were bought with the Lord's money, thus the car is under a curse. I would not want to ride in a car that is under a curse. Why do I say it's under a curse? Because Malachi 3:8-9 says if you withhold the tithe from God, you are under a curse for robbing Him. You might say, "Well, Dr. Williams, that's from the Old Testament and was part of the 'old' covenant." That's true, but in the New Testament, in 1 Corinthians, we read that what happened in the Old Testament is for our instruction. There is no exception made in the New Testament concerning our duty to tithe.

> **And concerning the tithe of the herd, or of the flock, even of whatsoever passeth under the rod, the tenth shall be holy unto the LORD.**
> **He shall not search whether it be good or bad . . . .**
> —**Leviticus 27:32-33a**

What does this mean? Simply this: let's say you came under a sudden temptation and you bought a lottery ticket. That's gambling, right? That is just as bad as a slot machine or a roulette wheel. Now, let's say you won a $10,000,000 jackpot. Well, your winnings are bad money.

But the Lord says, "I don't care if it is good or bad, the tithe is still mine." You ask, "How can I give this to the Lord? It's a lottery winning." God says you don't question whether it is good or bad, you give the tithe, because it belongs to God. The tenth belongs to the Lord; it's not ours. Whether it is bad earnings or good earnings doesn't matter; that is what God has instructed.

In other words, if old Uncle Vinnie, your gangster uncle, dies and leaves you fifty thousand dollars, and you know good and well it is "bad" money, the tithe still belongs to the Lord. He said bring the tithe whether it is good or bad. If you have ten crippled sheep, you've got to give God one of them even though it isn't perfect. It doesn't matter. The tithe belongs to the Lord.

But, we're told in the Bible the first fruit must be the first either in time, quality, or something that makes it outstanding and excellent. The Hebrews saw it as a promise that would come back to them.

It has to be the best and the first. It can't be the trash.

The tenth is a tithe but the first fruit is the first and the best. There is a difference between the two.

You don't have to bring a first fruit; you don't have to bring an offering; you don't have to give alms, and you don't have to make a faith promise. But if you spend God's money, which is the tithe, your finances will be under a curse. How do I know this? I know it because I believe God's Word, and have seen it in countless people's lives over the course of the past 35 years.

> Will a man rob God? Yet ye have robbed me. But ye say, Wherein have we robbed thee? In tithes and offerings.
> Ye are cursed with a curse: for ye have robbed me, even this whole nation.
> Bring ye all the tithes into the storehouse, that there may be meat in mine house, and prove me now herewith, saith the LORD of hosts, if I will not open you the windows of heaven, and pour you out a blessing, that there shall not be room enough to receive it.
> And I will rebuke the devourer for your sakes, and he shall not destroy the fruits of your ground; neither shall your vine cast her fruit before the time in the field, saith the LORD of hosts.
> And all nations shall call you blessed: for ye shall be a delightsome land, saith the LORD of hosts.
> —Malachi 3:8-12

Let's say you sold ten classic automobiles for $10,000 a piece. Now you've got $100,000, right? Now, you had originally invested $30,000 into those classic cars, making your profit $70,000. A tenth of your profit is the Lord's as the tithe, so $7,000 belongs to the Lord.

I would rather go without lights, and I'd rather go without gas than to go without bringing my tithe to the Lord, because it's His. Ten percent belongs to Him.

> **Anyone who can be trusted in little matters can also be trusted in important matters. But anyone who is dishonest in little matters will be dishonest in important matters.**
>
> **If you cannot be trusted with this wicked wealth, who will trust you with true wealth?**
>
> **And if you cannot be trusted with what belongs to someone else, who will give you something that will be your own?**
>
> **You cannot be the slave of two masters. You will like one more than the other or be more loyal to one than to the other. You cannot serve God and money.**
>
> **Luke 16:10-13 (CEV)**

If you cannot be trusted with earthly wealth, how can you be trusted with true spiritual wealth? And if you cannot be trusted with what belongs to someone else, who will give you something that will be your own?

The New Living Translation puts it this way: "If you are untrustworthy about worldly wealth, who will trust you with the riches of Heaven?"

IS GOD'S MONEY IN YOUR CLOSET?

If I come over to your house, will I see God's money hanging in your closet? "Here's my Armani, here's my Versace, and here's my Dior."

The first fruit and the tithe are not the same.

> **And [we obligate ourselves] to bring the firstfruits of our ground and the first of all the fruit of all trees year by year to the house of the Lord,**
>
> **As well as the firstborn of our sons and of our cattle, as is written in the Law, and the firstlings of our herds and flocks, to bring to the house of our God, to the priests who minister in [His] house.**

> And [we obligate ourselves] to bring the firstfruits of
> our ground and the first of all the fruit of all trees year
> by year to the house of the Lord,
> As well as the firstborn of our sons and of our cattle,
> as is written in the Law, and the firstlings of our herds
> and flocks, to bring to the house of our God, to the
> priests who minister in [His] house.
> And we shall bring the first and best of our coarse
> meal, our contributions, the fruit of all kinds of trees,
> of new wine, and of oil to the priests, to the chambers
> of the house of our God. And we shall bring the tithes
> from our ground to the Levites, for they, the Levites,
> collect the tithes in all our rural towns.
>
> —Nehemiah 10:35-37 (AMP)

Clearly we see the tithe and the first fruit are two different kinds of "seeds." The first fruit offering goes to those who
serve the Lord in ministry, and the tithe goes to the Lord
through the Levites, the people who handled the temple
finances.

Next, I'll show you how the first fruit offering can link
you up with a man of God's anointing.

"A first fruit offering is about getting a connection to someone else's anointing."

7

CONNECTING WITH THE ANOINTING

Some years ago, I was preaching at a ministers' conference when a young man walked up to me and said, "Pastor Dave, I am a pioneer pastor of an inner-city church. God led us to start a church."

I noticed he was talking just the opposite of the way most people who have needs talk.

He continued, "I read your book *Radical Riches*. I've seen that God has put His hand of anointing on you as a pastor and shown you how to make wise investments. It can be a challenge to get a missions church established and finding the money to do it. I need a miracle."

He then handed me a check for one thousand dollars made out to "Dave Williams."

I said, "Brother, I can't take this."

He shot back, "You have to take it because I need your anointing. Just wave it before the Lord and pray for me."

I was kind of embarrassed. Here's this young home missions pastor, struggling to get his church going, and he's giving me a thousand dollars I didn't need. But God spoke to me and said, "You don't need it, but he needs to give it to make a connection with your anointing." And so he gave me that thousand dollars, and of course it was a blessing and encouragement to me.

But the best blessing came just 18 months later. He sent me a note saying that since giving that first fruit offering and applying the principles in the book *Radical Riches*, "God has unlocked a miracle supply for me. I am now earning two hundred thousand dollars a year!" God started releasing ideas to him, and he launched a successful business he doesn't even have to run. His employees do all the work. He's earning two hundred thousand dollars from the business, and it is supporting the new church while it grows. And yes, he teaches those people the principles of sowing and reaping.

A first fruit offering is about getting a connection to someone else's anointing.

I mentioned to you that after I heard the first fruit teaching, I immediately sent the preacher who taught it the entire check that was given to me for attending that meeting.

What happened afterward? This has never happened before—never. The next Tuesday evening, I was teaching my Pacesetting Leadership class, and one particular student was acting fidgety. Finally, at the end of the class, she ran outside and then ran back in.

"Pastor," she said, "I don't know why, but God's been speaking to me during this class and telling me to give you this. She handed me sixty dollars."

I said. "I can't take this."

She said, "You have to take it. God told me to give it to you."

So I prayed over it and over her, "God, in the name of Jesus let her barns overflow and her vats overflow with fresh ideas like new wine from Heaven."

Another man came up to me that same night and said, "Pastor Williams, I've got to give you this. I have a need in my life, and I need a connection with your anointing." He handed me a check for three hundred dollars.

That same night, when I went back to my office (before I ever taught on the miracle breakthrough power of the first fruit) I heard a knock on my door. When I opened it, a couple was standing there. The man said, "I have to talk to you pastor. We are going into the ministry, and we really need your anointing, so we want to give you this." He handed me an envelope.

I said, "Come on, you know I don't need this."

"You may not need it, Pastor Dave," he responded, "but we need a connection with your anointing." I opened the envelope and inside was two thousand dollars!

I begged, "Please take this back."

He said, "Just wave it before the Lord and send your anointing my way." I started waving it before the Lord and prayed for anointing on them. I prayed that all their storehouses would be blessed and their vats would overflow.

Have you noticed that Creflo Dollar sounds a lot like Kenneth Copeland? Do you know that Creflo planted financial seeds into Kenneth Copeland's ministry? Before long, Creflo came out of obscurity and is now one of America's most famous pastors. However, it didn't happen until he released the first fruit; then he got a connection with Ken's anointing.

You don't get a connection with a person's anointing by simply mailing in prayer requests. It's the first fruit offering that brings the connection.

In the Bible, God talks about bringing the first fruit to the priest in Numbers:

> **And the LORD spake unto Aaron, Behold, I also have given thee the charge of mine heave offerings of all the hallowed things of the children of Israel; unto thee have I given them by reason of the anointing and to thy sons, by an ordinance for ever.**
> **—Numbers 18:8**

What God said to Aaron was this: The first fruit offering is to be an ordinance that goes on forever and ever. It's the law of the first fruit. You bring the first fruit to the priest (the minister, the pastor, the evangelist, the missionary, etc.). He, in turn, waves it before the Lord and prays like this:

"Lord, accept this offering from this dear, precious child of Yours. Put your blessing over his home, send an angel ahead of him, and bring him into the place you have prepared for him. Loose healing upon his home and upon his life, and let my anointing be imparted to him."

As I mentioned earlier in this book, I don't think Numbers 18:8 can be used as a proof text for getting a connection with an anointing. Nonetheless, the principle is found throughout God's Word. You plant "seed" into a certain type of ground and your harvest has a "connection" with all the nutrients in that particular soil.

Mary Jo and I have practiced this for years without really calling it "first fruits." We just knew we should invest into the personal lives of people who have been our leaders in some way, and those whose anointing we'd like to share.

I have always believed if you really want someone's anointing you have to plant something into that person's life.

Ministers often find people coming to them and asking, "Will you share your anointing with me? Will you lay hands on me?"

Well, the way you can actually get a harvest of their anointing is when you plant first fruit offerings into their lives. When you plant seed in mineral rich soil, the harvest soaks up those minerals. It's your harvest. Plant your first fruit seeds wisely in good ground.

There was a day when God's people became careless about where they planted their "seeds," and then wondered why their crops were so bad, or worse yet, nonexistent.

For they have sown the wind, and they shall reap the whirlwind: it hath no stalk; the bud shall yield no meal: if so be it yield, the strangers shall swallow it up.
—Hosea 8:7

When you honor the Lord with the first fruits of all your increase, not only will your storehouses start to overflow, but your vats will overflow too. The ideas for income, increase, and growth come like a flood to your mind and heart. That's what happened to the missionary pastor in Detroit when he released that first fruit to the "priest." I was the representative of the priesthood. After he released it, suddenly the miracle breakthrough ideas for his business flooded his mind. Probably most people would love to have a two hundred thousand dollar a year income. That is his income and increase. Can you imagine his tithe now?

ENCOURAGING THE LORD'S SERVANTS

> Moreover he commanded the people that dwelt in Jerusalem to give the portion of the priests and the Levites, that they might be encouraged in the law of the LORD.
> And as soon as the commandment came abroad, the children of Israel brought in abundance the first-fruits of corn, wine, and oil, and honey, and of all the increase of the field; and the tithe of all things brought they in abundantly.
>
> —2 Chronicles 31:4-5

Once again, notice the distinction between the tithe and first fruit offering.

The Levites were the "helps" ministers of their day. Priests who worked in the temples were like today's pastors. The people brought first fruit gifts to the priests and Levites to encourage them in the law of the Lord.

It says in verse six, they laid the first fruits and the tithes by heaps. When is the last time you laid heaps of encouragement at a man of God's feet?

> And concerning the children of Israel and Judah, that dwelt in the cities of Judah, they also brought in the tithe of oxen and sheep, and the tithe of holy things which were consecrated unto the LORD their God, and laid them by heaps.
>
> —2 Chronicles 31:6

The people brought the first fruits and lay them in heaps at the priests and Levites' feet so that they were encouraged in the work and Word of the Lord. They always encouraged others in the Word of the Lord, but they needed encouragement themselves sometimes.

Rarely does a layperson realize the enormous task ministers undertake. Ministers face misunderstandings, attacks, and betrayals. They deal with all kinds of unpleasant things. At the same time, they must maintain their own spiritual lives for the sake of the people they serve. Very few understand the real commitment of true men and women of God. They need someone who really wants a connection with their anointing. That is encouraging to them.

In 2 Kings 4, there is a true story of a woman who encouraged a man of God in a tangible and practical way. It caused her to step into the realm of miracles. Let's read it:

> One day Elisha went to the town of Shunem. A wealthy woman lived there, and she urged him to come to her home for a meal. After that, whenever he passed that way, he would stop there for something to eat.
>
> She said to her husband, "I am sure this man who stops in from time to time is a holy man of God.
>
> "Let's build a small room for him on the roof and furnish it with a bed, a table, a chair, and a lamp. Then he will have a place to stay whenever he comes by."
>
> One day Elisha returned to Shunem, and he went up to this upper room to rest. He said to his servant Gehazi, "Tell the woman from Shunem I want to speak to her." When she appeared,
>
> Elisha said to Gehazi, "Tell her, 'We appreciate the kind concern you have shown us. What can we do for you? Can we put in a good word for you to the king or to the commander of the army?'" "No," she replied, "my family takes good care of me."
>
> Later Elisha asked Gehazi, "What can we do for her?" Gehazi replied, "She doesn't have a son, and her husband is an old man."

"Call her back again," Elisha told him. When the
woman returned, Elisha said to her as she stood in the
doorway,

"Next year at this time you will be holding a son in
your arms!"

"No, my lord!" she cried. "O man of God, don't
deceive me and get my hopes up like that."

But sure enough, the woman soon became pregnant.
And at that time the following year she had a son, just
as Elisha had said.

One day when her child was older, he went out to
help his father, who was working with the harvesters.

Suddenly he cried out, "My head hurts! My head
hurts!" His father said to one of the servants, "Carry
him home to his mother."

So the servant took him home, and his mother held
him on her lap. But around noontime he died.

She carried him up and laid him on the bed of the
man of God, then shut the door and left him there.

She sent a message to her husband: "Send one of the
servants and a donkey so that I can hurry to the man
of God and come right back."

"Why go today?" he asked. "It is neither a new
moon festival nor a Sabbath." But she said, "It will be
all right."

So she saddled the donkey and said to the servant,
"Hurry! Don't slow down unless I tell you to."

As she approached the man of God at Mount
Carmel, Elisha saw her in the distance. He said to
Gehazi, "Look, the woman from Shunem is coming.

Run out to meet her and ask her, 'Is everything all
right with you, your husband, and your child?'" "Yes,"
the woman told Gehazi, "everything is fine."

But when she came to the man of God at the moun-
tain, she fell to the ground before him and caught
hold of his feet. Gehazi began to push her away, but
the man of God said, "Leave her alone. She is deeply
troubled, but the LORD has not told me what it is."

Then she said, "Did I ask you for a son, my lord? And
didn't I say, 'Don't deceive me and get my hopes up'?"

Then Elisha said to Gehazi, "Get ready to travel;
take my staff and go! Don't talk to anyone along the

way. Go quickly and lay the staff on the child's face."

But the boy's mother said, "As surely as the LORD lives and you yourself live, I won't go home unless you go with me." So Elisha returned with her.

Gehazi hurried on ahead and laid the staff on the child's face, but nothing happened. There was no sign of life. He returned to meet Elisha and told him, "The child is still dead."

When Elisha arrived, the child was indeed dead, lying there on the prophet's bed.

He went in alone and shut the door behind him and prayed to the Lord.

Then he lay down on the child's body, placing his mouth on the child's mouth, his eyes on the child's eyes, and his hands on the child's hands. And as he stretched out on him, the child's body began to grow warm again!

Elisha got up, walked back and forth across the room once, and then stretched himself out again on the child. This time the boy sneezed seven times and opened his eyes!

Then Elisha summoned Gehazi. "Call the child's mother!" he said. And when she came in, Elisha said, "Here, take your son!"

She fell at his feet and bowed before him, overwhelmed with gratitude. Then she took her son in her arms and carried him downstairs.

—2 Kings 4:8-37 (NLT)

By blessing and encouraging the man of God, she moved into the realm of Elisha's miracles. First, she gave birth to a son after being barren all her life. Second, when she needed a family miracle, it was available because she had a connection with Elisha.

SETTING THE STAGE FOR YOUR FUTURE

When the home missions pastor I told you about released a huge "seed" into my life, he was setting the stage for his own successful future. The first fruit is "a promise to come." Do you know what many missionaries and new pastors do? They reason, "Why should I give him anything? He ought to be giving to me. He doesn't need my offering."

Do you know what that is? It's a poverty mentality. Success will usually be just out of reach for people who think like that. "Someone ought to be giving to me," the poverty spirit says. But God's Spirit, unlike the spirit of this world, says, "Give and it shall be given unto you . . . ."

What would we be without spiritual fathers and people who have led us in the "Way" and taught us along the way?

You don't plant first fruit seed because the person you give it to needs it. You do it to honor and worship the Lord, to encourage the man or woman of God, and to get a connection with his or her anointing.

BLESSING OUR SPIRITUAL FATHERS

For many years, I sent Pastor Glenn Snook money as an investment in him as one of my spiritual fathers. And it was a significant amount. I never took a tax deduction because it was given to him personally. He always had this unique ability to take complicated truths and make them simple for people to understand. I wanted that anointing.

We need to remember, once again, the priests were paid from the people's tithe. That was their salary. A first fruit offering was a special blessing just for them and their families.

Then there is Ivar Frick; he was the Assemblies of God district superintendent when I started in ministry. He is in his nineties now. Every year Mary Jo and I send him money because he always had an anointing to talk about Jesus in a simple way. I wanted that anointing in my ministry.

We've given personal first fruit offerings to a pastor in Costa Mesa. He is a real Bible teacher. I wanted that anointing. We've given first fruits to Pastor Tommy Barnett, Dr. Oral Roberts and a few others I respect deeply. And I've reaped a supernatural partnership with these men, sharing in their unique anointings.

These were personal gifts, not tax deductible and not for the ministry, but gifts to them.

You don't share a person's anointing by imitating them. You share their anointing by investing in them through the miracle breakthrough power of the first fruit offering.

I have no hidden motivation in teaching this. I really don't. My church is incredibly good to me; I am paid well. Yet I know I am on my way to a greater wealthy place, so I can give even more to missions. I am planting "seeds" and first fruits now more than ever.

ALMS GO TO THE NEEDY. FIRST FRUITS DO NOT—EVER!

You have to understand this: We don't give just because somebody needs it; that's alms. You will gain a little interest, but you will never get into the wealthy place by just giving alms. I have heard people say, "I heard of this pastor and he's been struggling for fifteen years. He can't keep his Church together, it's always falling apart, everything bad happens to him. Well, I'm just going to write out a check and help that pastor out."

Is that the anointing you want a connection with? When you give to someone in need, that's not a first fruit but alms. That is benevolence, a loan to the Lord, when you help someone who is struggling. With the first fruit offering, however, you're planting some seed, and the harvest you get will depend on where you plant your seed.

Many of the ministers I've given first fruit offerings to didn't need the money. They simply needed encouragement, and I needed their anointing.

> **And the LORD spake unto Aaron, Behold, I also have given thee the charge of mine heave offerings of all the hallowed things of the children of Israel; unto thee have I given them by reason of the anointing, and to thy sons, by an ordinance for ever.**
>
> **—Numbers 18:8**

Heave offerings and first fruit offerings are apparently the same. When a man of God received a first fruit offering he would wave it before the Lord, making it acceptable and pronouncing the blessing over the home of the giver.

King David, after having great success in taking back the city of Ziklag and taking a great plunder from the enemy, remembered to share a first fruit with the elders and leaders.

> **When he arrived at Ziklag, David sent part of the plunder to the elders of Judah, who were his friends. "Here is a present for you, taken from the Lord's enemies," he said.**
>
> **—1 Samuel 30:26 (NLT)**

I always plant first fruit seeds where I can get a connection to the anointing.

What you make happen for the man of God, God will make happen for you. It will all flow down eventually.

> It is like the precious ointment upon the head, that ran down upon the beard, even Aaron's beard: that went down to the skirts of his garments;
> As the dew of Hermon, and as the dew that descended upon the mountains of Zion: for there the LORD commanded the blessing, even life for evermore.
>
> —Psalm 133:2-3

"Whenever we start trying to figure out—to the penny—what we have to do instead of what we have the joyous privilege of doing, it becomes a legalistic bondage."

8

THE MIRACLE BREAKTHROUGH POWER

A young minister, was sitting in our church service several years ago, when he said the Lord told him to plant a seed of $10,000 into my life. I didn't ask for it; I didn't expect it, and I didn't even need it. But he obeyed the Lord and began—week-after-week—sending me "first fruit" offerings until he had given the full amount. I felt strange about this, but I didn't want to cheat him out of a successful future and a promise to come.

He testified that within three months, his net assets went up one hundred thousand dollars. Now, just a few years later, he owns all kinds of premiere properties, conducts successful miracle services around the country, and has enjoyed blessing after blessing in both his home and in his investments. He attributes it all to outrageous giving to the Lord and the Lord's servants.

The first fruit carries the miracle breakthrough power from heaven to earth.

Money was meant to serve you. You were never meant to serve money. There are many people who violate the first four commandments. The first four commandments involve our relationship to God and they are all about putting God first in everything.

GET THE BLESSING

Again I want to look at three different translations to help you get a clear picture. Read them carefully.

> And the first of all the firstfruits of all kinds, and every offering of all kinds from all your offerings, shall belong to the priests. You shall also give to the priest the first of your coarse meal and bread dough, that a blessing may rest on your house.
>
> —Ezekiel 44:30 (AMP)

> And the first of all the firstfruits of all things, and every oblation of all, of every sort of your oblations, shall be the priest's: ye shall also give unto the priest the first of your dough, that he may cause the blessing to rest in thine house.
>
> —Ezekiel 44:30

> The first part of every harvest will belong to the priests. They will also receive part of all special gifts and offerings the Israelites bring to me. And whenever any of my people bake bread, they will give their first loaf as an offering to the priests, and I will bless the homes of the people when they do this.
>
> —Ezekiel 44:30 (CEV)

The man or woman of God can cause the blessing to rest on your home. That's powerful. Yet so many treat the minister disgracefully—with contempt and sarcasm—because they don't believe in the miracle breakthrough power of the first fruit.

> And this shall be the priest's due from the people, from those who offer a sacrifice, whether it be ox or

sheep: they shall give to the priest the shoulder and the two cheeks and the stomach.

The firstfruits of your grain, of your new wine, and of your oil, and the first or best of the fleece of your sheep you shall give the priest.

For the Lord your God has chosen him out of all your tribes to stand to minister in the name [and presence] of the Lord, him and his sons forever.

And if a Levite comes from any of your towns out of all Israel where he is a temporary resident, he may come whenever he desires to [the sanctuary] the place the Lord will choose;

Then he may minister in the name [and presence of] the Lord his God like all his brethren the Levites who stand to minister there before the Lord.

They shall have equal portions to eat, besides what may come of the sale of his patrimony.

—Deuteronomy 18:3-8 (AMP)

Ask yourself these questions now, and answer them honestly:

- Do you want overflowing storehouses?
- Do you want revelation from heaven to burst forth upon your life?
- Do you want your home to possess the blessing?
- Do want the Angel of the Lord going ahead of you?
- Do you want God to be an enemy to your enemies?
- Do you want to honor the Lord in a practical way, while encouraging those who serve the Lord?
- Do you want a connection with someone's anointing? Maybe it's an intercessor (that's a priest), or someone in the helps ministry around the church.
- Do you want to break bondages in your life and in other's lives?

- Do you want the missing link in God's system of wealth?
- Do you want to break the spirit of poverty, mediocrity, and stagnation?

If you said "Yes!" to these questions, find someone whose anointing you want to link with and plant your first fruit. Do it in faith. Remember some spiritual "father" you haven't blessed or encouraged in a long time and release a first fruit to him or her.

And please . . . don't make this a rigid, joyless, legalistic matter. Whenever someone asks me, "Do I have to give a first fruit on a bonus or a sale of a car," and the questions go on and on, I tell them, "You don't have to do anything." Whenever we start trying to figure out—to the penny—what we have to do instead of what we have the joyous privilege of doing, it becomes a legalistic bondage.

My daughter, Trina Lee, lives in Nashville, Tennessee. Recently, I phoned her and we were talking about the blessing of the first fruit. She got all excited and couldn't wait to start. She told me she had a check she hadn't cashed yet—the first one from one of her businesses—and she wanted to give it as a first fruit. She gave it to a woman who has prayed for her for years. This woman has a great anointing to intercede and to teach God's Word in an uncomplicated and motivational way. So Trina sent it to her along with an encouraging note.

I'm so excited about her future and yours.

The first fruit is about your future. It is a "promise to come."

"Receive the blessing. It's found in the miracle breakthrough power of the first fruit."

9

CLOSING WORDS AND A PRAYER FOR YOU

Let me share a quick review of the principles of the first fruit offering so you don't miss a great blessing in your future:

- The first fruit encourages those who work for the Lord (2 Chronicles 31:4-6).
- The first fruit connects you with God's anointing on His servants (Numbers 18:8).
- The first fruit brings blessings to your home and family (Ezekiel 44:30).
- The first fruit ensures that the rest of your increase will be holy (Romans 11:16).
- The first fruit shows that you honor the Lord (Proverbs 3:9).
- The first fruit releases an angel to go before you to lead you into the place God has prepared for you (Exodus 23:20; Psalm 66:12).
- The first fruit looses destruction on your personal enemies (debt, lack, poverty, bondage, etc.).

- The first fruit releases God's healing power and longevity in your life. (Exodus 23:22, 25, 26).

The term "first fruits" to the Hebrew meant, "a promise to come." When God's people brought their first fruit offering, they understood it was for their own future, as Solomon said in Proverbs 3:9-10 ("barns overflowing, vats bursting forth").

If you are a servant of Jesus Christ and receive a first fruit offering from someone, this is a good prayer to pray as you wave the offering before the Lord:

> *In Jesus' Name, I now wave this offering before the Lord, making it acceptable and bringing the blessing over your home. I pray that you will be filled with fresh revelation and anointing, your storage places will overflow with everything good, that your life be advanced, enlargement become a reality, your enemies be defeated, and that Jesus Christ will be glorified in and through your work, witness, and ministry . . . now and forevermore.*
>
> *Amen!*

Receive the blessing. It's found in the miracle breakthrough power of the first fruit.

About Dave Williams, D.Min.

Dave Williams is pastor of Mount Hope Church and International Outreach Ministries with headquarters in Lansing, Michigan. He has pastored there for over 27 years, leading the church from 226 to over 4,000 members today.

The ministry campus comprises 60 acres in Delta Township, Michigan, and includes a worship center, Bible Training Institute, children's center, youth facilities, Garden Prayer Chapel, Global Prayer Center, Gym and Fitness Center, Care facilities, and a medical complex.

Construction of Gilead Healing Center was completed in 2003. It is a multi-million dollar edifice that includes medical facilities, nutritional education, and fitness training. Its most important mission is to equip believers to minister to the sick as Jesus and His disciples did. Medical and osteopathic doctors, doctors of chiropractic and naturopathy, and licensed physical and massage therapists all work harmoniously with trained prayer partners to bring about miraculous healing for suffering people from all over the United States.

Under Dave's leadership, 43 daughter and branch churches have been successfully planted in Michigan, the Philippines, Ghana, Ivory Coast, and Zimbabwe. Including all branch churches, Mount Hope Churches claim over 14,000 members as of December 2005.

Dave is founder and president of Mount Hope Bible Training Institute, a fully accredited, church-based leadership institute for training ministers, church planters, and lay people to perform the work of the ministry. Dave established and leads the Dave Williams School for Church Planters, located in St. Pete Beach, Florida.

He has authored 63 books including fifteen-time bestseller, *The New Life . . . The Start of Something Wonderful* (with over 2 million books sold in eight languages). More recently, he authored *The World Beyond: The Mysteries of Heaven and How to Get There* (over 100,000 copies sold). *Radical Riches* was a Barnes and Noble top seller for 10 consecutive months. His *Miracle Results of Fasting* (Harrison House Publishers) was an Amazon.com five-star top seller for two years in a row.

Dave's articles and reviews have appeared in national magazines such as *Advance, Pentecostal Evangel, Charisma, Ministries Today, Lansing Magazine, Detroit Free Press, World News*, and others.

According to the Nielsen ratings, Dave's television program, *The Pacesetter's Path*, is the number one viewed religious program on both ABC and CBS affiliates in Michigan. He has appeared on national television in the United States and Canada, and has been heard worldwide over Billy Graham's "Decision Network." His television ministry is viewed worldwide over eleven satellite systems and is broadcast 44 times weekly.

Along with his wife, Mary Jo, Dave established The Dave and Mary Jo Williams Charitable Mission (Strategic Global Mission), a non-profit foundation providing scholarships to pioneer pastors and ministry students, as well as grants to inner-city children's ministries.

Dave, as a private pilot, flies for fun. He and Mary Jo have two grown children and live in Delta Township, Michigan.

CONTACT INFORMATION

Mount Hope Church and International Outreach Ministries
202 S. Creyts Road
Lansing, Michigan 48917

For a complete list of Dave Williams' life-changing
books, CDs and videos call:

Phone: 517-321-2780
800-888-7284
TDD: 517-321-8200

or go to our web site:
www.mounthopechurch.org

For prayer requests, call the
Mount Hope Global Prayer Center
24-hour prayer line at:
517-327-PRAY
(517-327-7729)

3 LIFE-CHANGING BOOKS
BY DAVE WILLIAMS

EMERGING LEADERS—They are wall breakers and city takers! Don't try to stop them. They are unstoppable. Don't try to understand them. They are often unorthodox in their approach. They are . . . EMERGING LEADERS—a new breed of church leadership for the 21st century, and you can be one of them! $12.⁹⁵

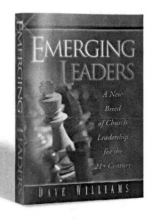

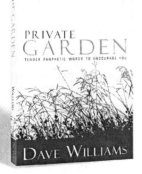

PRIVATE GARDEN   In this book Pastor Dave Williams shares encouraging prophetic words the Holy Spirit has spoken into his life and ministry. As you read, you will receive Holy Spirit encouragement and direction.

$12.⁹⁵

COMING INTO THE WEALTHY PLACE— God wants you to be able to "abound to every good work." You need to learn how to release God's power in your life to get wealth. This book will show you how to go through the door of just good enough into *The Wealthy Place!* $14.⁹⁵

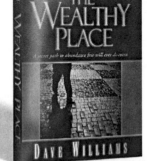

If you enjoyed reading *Miracle Breakthrough Power of the First Fruit*, you will enjoy reading *Coming Into the Wealthy Place*, also by Dr. Dave Williams. For an excerpt continue reading . . . .

CHASING RAINBOWS

Twenty some years ago, a young member of our church, graduated from Oral Roberts University and had no idea what he was going to do with his life. He began applying God's principles of wealth, and in a recent year his business achieved $43 million in gross sales.

Another young man didn't have much going for him when he started out 10 years ago. He wasn't properly educated, yet he put into motion God's radical wealth principles, and last year his tithe (10 percent of his income) was more than $50,000.

Some people find the wealthy place, but many more never do. If life was a hotel, they live on level one, two, or even three, and they think that is as good as it gets. But those first levels are just the beginning. The top floor is the concierge level where service is outstanding and everyone around is anxious to meet your every need. Yes, there is much more than just "getting by" for us, brother or sister! Christians should be moving up to higher and higher levels of wealth and responsibility, managing the resources God has put into this earth as the men in my examples have done.

I no longer understand why anyone is content with little. A typical married man works one or more jobs, and his wife also works. They have a house in the suburbs and own two cars. They think they're happy. They think they're prospering, but they are not. They are in poverty because they spend their lives chasing dollars instead of having dollars chase them.

They are on the first floor working themselves to death and knowing nothing about life on the concierge level. He has to work two jobs, and his wife has to work as well just to keep up their so-called "middle class" lifestyle. The kids don't know their parents, and the family never knows true wealth. They are living in a form of poverty!

When I talk about the wealthy place, I'm talking about the outrageous wealth God is willing to pour into His people. The more revelation God gives me about money, the more radical and determined I get! You, and every other Christian, should insist on moving up to the top floor and having money chase you instead of the other way around. I have been on the first floor, the concierge level, and everything in between, and I'm convinced that the wealthy place is where all Christians belong.

PIPE DREAMS

In the introduction of my book, *Radical Riches*, I told the story of when I was eight years old. It was close to the fourth of July, and I wanted to find the pot of gold at the end of the rainbow. I wanted some money to buy firecrackers—Roman candles, ladyfingers, M-80s, silver salutes, cherry bombs, you name it. One day my friends and I disobeyed our parents and followed a rainbow for six miles but never found that pot of gold. We were disappointed, deflated, and our pockets were as empty as when we began.

That's a picture of the life many people choose to lead. They chase rainbows, thinking they're going to find a pot of gold. They go after lotteries, casinos, good-luck charms, and get-rich-quick schemes.

I pastor a church with more than 4,000 members, and 70 percent of the prayer requests I get every week pertain to financial problems. You wouldn't believe what people write:

"Pray that I will be able to refinance my house so I can pay off my credit cards."

"Pray that the bank will approve our new home equity line of credit."

"Pray that I will get financing for my new car."

"Pray that I will have enough income so I can start tithing."

I sometimes want to stamp a big "STUPID" on the card and send it back to the person who submitted it. Then I remember, I was in the same place for many years of my life!

It's painfully clear that people don't know how to handle money unless they are taught. God said:

My people are destroyed for lack of knowledge. . .
—Hosea 4:6a

Wealth and knowledge are not found in rainbows, lotteries, casinos, or good luck. They are not even found in prayer requests that ask God to bless the mismanagement of money.

A man came to our office not long ago and asked for $300 from our Benevolence Fund. An associate minister sat with him and listened as the man explained that his $270 paycheck had been stolen. He was asking for $300 because he said the Lord wanted to bless him. The minister asked how he had lost the money, and he said a prostitute stole it from him while he was witnessing to her. The minister asked how it happened, and he said, "I was in a room witnessing to a prostitute, and another prostitute in the room next door took the money out of my pants." This guy was caught with his pants down! He had handled money and morality poorly and lost what he had. We didn't give him any money.

We've all done stupid things before (though maybe not *that* stupid). I'm sure you can point to money mistakes in your own past. I sure can.

I was with my family in the Bahamas. One morning, we went to the beautiful Atlantis Hotel where you can walk through the Plexiglas tunnels and see sharks swimming around you. There are amazing beaches and pools, and nobody else was around. The other guests, I suppose, had spent the night gambling and drinking, so they were sleeping in.

We passed by the casino. I had always wanted to try a slot machine, but I didn't want my mom (who was vacationing with us) to know. And I certainly didn't want my wife or kids to know either. So I took my time and hung back until they were out of sight. Then I ducked in and put a quarter in a slot machine. I pulled the handle, the wheels clicked into place, and the machine started ringing and flashing. Money poured out, plunk, plunk, plunk, plunk, plunk! The sound of the coins hitting the steel tray was almost deafening.

Everyone turned around and looked at me. I saw my mother, hands on her hips, and my wife Mary Jo rolling her eyes. My kids were both laughing. I was humiliated. It was fun for a moment, but that's not the door to the wealthy place! I could pull slots all of my life and never get another return. People who believe that gambling is the answer just slide deeper and deeper into financial hell.

THE POWER TO GET WEALTH

The Bible gives all kinds of signs directing us to the wealthy place. Deuteronomy 8:18 says:

> But thou shalt remember the LORD thy God: for it is he that giveth thee power to get wealth, that he may establish his covenant which he sware unto thy fathers, as it is this day.

God is not careless in what He says. He means every word. He said clearly that He has given you and me the power to get wealth. Ephesians 3:20 confirms this:

> Unto him, who is able to do exceedingly abundant above all that we could ask or think according to the power that worketh in us.

God has given His children the power—not the skill or talent, necessarily, but the *power*—to get wealth, and the amount of wealth we enjoy in this life will be according to our management of the wealth He entrusts to us right now.

Printed in the United States
126966LV00002B/313-1500/P